Living Things

How Plants and Animals Work

DEVELOPED IN COOPERATION

WITH

THE SCIENCE PLACE

DALLAS, TEXAS

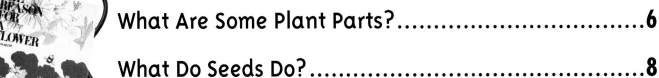

Living Things

A living thing has structures that work together
to help it survive in its environment.

Read-Aloud

Living Things

VIDEO

Plants and animals are living things which meet
their different basic needs in different ways.

Different kinds of plants have different structures
that help them meet their needs. These structures are
adapted to their environments.

Literature

JUL 0 4 2002

Different kinds of animals have different structures that help them meet their needs. Their structures are adapted to their environments.

What Did We Learn?

THE
BABY
ZOO
BRUCE
McMILLAN

...erature

What Are Plants and Animals?

There are millions of different kinds of plants and animals living in the world around you.

You need:
Hand lens
Crayons or markers

My
Science
Book

Find a plant or animal.

❶ Look for a living thing. Is it a plant or an animal?

❷ Use your hand lens. How many different parts of your plant or animal do you see? How do you think your living thing uses each of these parts?

❸ Draw or write about the parts you saw.

Living things grow. They need air, water, and food. Living things make new young. What parts help plants do these things? What parts help animals do these things?

THINK!
Are you a plant or an animal?

5

What Are Some Plant Parts?

Plants are living things. What parts do plants have? What do you think each part does for the plant? How can people use these parts?

Flowers

Seeds

Roots

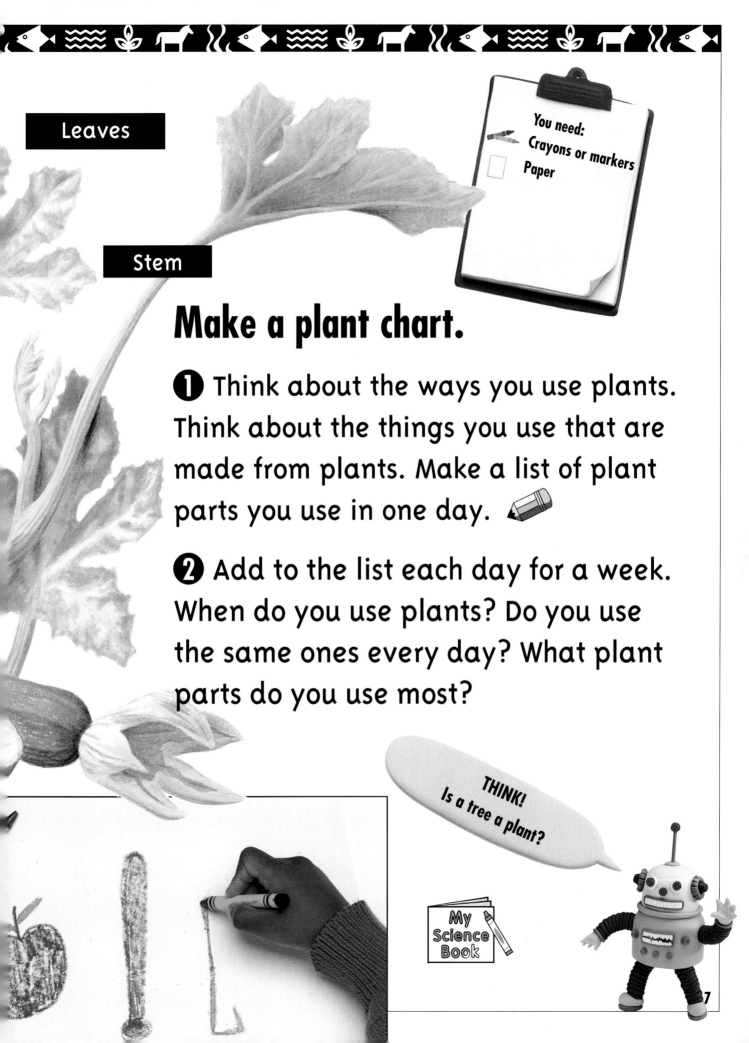

Leaves

Stem

Make a plant chart.

❶ Think about the ways you use plants. Think about the things you use that are made from plants. Make a list of plant parts you use in one day.

❷ Add to the list each day for a week. When do you use plants? Do you use the same ones every day? What plant parts do you use most?

THINK!
Is a tree a plant?

My Science Book

What Do Seeds Do?

Seeds are one part of a plant. Seeds can grow into new plants. What will different seeds grow into?

Apple seeds are black and smooth. They will only grow into apple trees.

Pumpkin seeds are large and pale and flat. They will only grow into pumpkin plants.

Plant mystery seeds.

You need:
Mystery seeds
Plastic cup
Soil
Paper towel strip

❶ Line the cup with the paper towel and fill it with soil.

❷ Slide two mystery seeds between the paper towel and the cup. Put more seeds in the soil and cover them.

❸ Water the seeds. Check them every day for one week. What happens?

THINK!
What part of your mystery plant do you think you'll see first?

9

What Do Roots Do?

Roots are an important part of most plants.

You need:
Mystery plants
Toothpicks
Hand lens
Construction paper

Observe roots.

❶ Look at your plants. Dig one up.

❷ Put the plant on paper. Look at a root with your hand lens.

❸ Wait two days. Look at a root in your cup. Does it look different now? How can you tell the roots are growing?

Plants need to get water and minerals from the soil. How do you think roots help plants do this? What else do roots do?

THINK!
What plant roots do people eat?

What Do Stems Do?

Roots get water and minerals from the soil. What do you think stems do? Look at your plants. Can you find their stems?

You need:
Plastic cups
Water
Food coloring
Eye dropper
Celery stalks

Test stem action.

❶ Put water and food coloring in one cup and leave another cup empty. Stick one piece of celery in each cup.

❷ Wait one hour. What happens? What do stems do for a plant?

One thing stems do is help hold leaves up to the light. Are all plant stems tall and thin? What are some different kinds of stems?

THINK!
How are minerals in the soil like your food coloring?

What Do Leaves Do?

Water travels through the stems to the leaves. Leaves use sunlight to change air and water into food. Some of the food flows into the rest of the plant.

You need:
Mystery plants
Boxes

Test your plants in sunlight.

1 Set up your mystery plants as in the photo below.

2 Observe the plants every day for one week. What do you learn about your plants?

THINK!
What do plants do that animals can't do?

When plants make food they give off oxygen. What needs oxygen to live?

15

What Are Some Animal Parts?

Like plants, animals are living things. They need air, food, and water to live.

Grizzly bears eat fish. What body parts help them find the fish? What parts help them catch the fish and eat?

Grizzly bears can run very fast. What body parts help them move?

Grizzlies live in the cold northern woods.
What body parts help them stay warm?

My Science Book

THINK!
What body parts
do you think help a
grizzly bear breathe?

How Do Animals Get Air?

Plants give off oxygen into the air. Animals need oxygen to live. Many animals have lungs and breathe as you do.

Whales and dolphins live in the water, but they aren't fish. They come to the top to breathe air.

Fish can stay under water all the time. Instead of lungs, they have body parts called gills. Gills get oxygen from the water.

You need:
Plastic cups
Cold water
Hand lens

Find air in water.

❶ Look at a cup of water that has been sitting out overnight.

❷ Put a fresh cup of water next to it.

❸ Look at the cups with your hand lens. How do you explain what you see?

THINK!
What will happen if you leave the second cup of water standing overnight?

How Do Animals Eat?

All living things need food. Plants make
their own food but animals don't.
Animals need to drink water and eat food.
Some animals eat plants. Some animals
eat other animals.

Butterflies sip the sweet
liquid from flowers. Their
mouths are made
for sucking.

Chameleons eat flying insects. Their tongues are
long and sticky, and flick out to catch insects.

Many animals have teeth. Some teeth are for grinding. Buffalo use their teeth for grinding grass and leaves.

Some teeth are for cutting and tearing. Lions use their sharp teeth to eat meat.

Have you seen other animals eating? What kind of mouths do they have?

THINK!
What do you eat?
What kind of teeth do you have?

How Do Animals Move?

Animals move to find food and to get away from danger. What parts help animals move?

A kangaroo's legs and feet help make it a great jumper.

A monkey uses its hands and feet to swing through trees.

Some animals, like snails and fish, have no legs. How do they move?

Move like animals.

❶ Choose an animal you like.

❷ Show how your animal moves.

THINK!
What body parts help you move?

How Do Animals See?

Animals use their senses to move and find food. How do animals use their sense of sight?

Some animals have eyes that can see at night. Owls can look for food in the dark.

Each of your eyes has one part called a lens. A fly's eye has many lenses to see things moving all around it.

You need:
Straws
Tape
Cardboard tube

See what a fly sees.

❶ Tape your straws together and slide them inside the tube.

❷ Look through the tube. Do things look different?

THINK!
Why do you think eyelids and eyelashes are important?

How Do Animals Smell and Hear?

What other senses do animals have?
What parts help them use these senses?

Some animals, like these puppies, use
their noses to find their mother's milk
before their eyes are open.

Some animals use their ears
to help protect themselves.
This rabbit can hear danger
coming from far away.

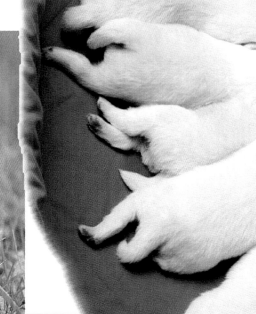

You need:
Construction paper
Paper cups
Scissors
Tape

Catch some sound.

❶ Think about the ears of some different animals. How big are they? What shapes are they?

❷ Now make your own sound catchers and try them on. Listen to quiet sounds. Trade sound catchers so you can try different kinds.

Which sound catchers work best for you?

THINK!
How do you use your senses of smell and hearing?

What Do Animal Body Coverings Do?

What kinds of body coverings do these animals have? How do their body coverings help them?

What makes some animals hard to see?
How do you think this helps them?

You need:
Newspaper
Black, white and
    red construction
    paper
Scissors

Pick up the pieces.

❶ Cut newspaper and construction paper into many small pieces.

❷ Tape big sheets of newspaper to the floor and drop the paper pieces onto it.

❸ Have a race. Who can pick up their pieces the fastest? Why?

THINK!
What special
coverings do
plants have?

What Plants and Animals Live Around You?

No matter where you live, plants and animals live there, too.

What plants can you find? What parts do they have? What animals can you find? How do their parts help them stay alive?

How are you like the plants and animals around you?

You need:
Milk carton
String
Scissors
Sticks
Birdseed

Make a bird feeder to see birds up close. What birds come to your feeder?

How do the different birds eat? How do they use their body parts?

What part of the plant does the birdseed come from? What else do birds eat?

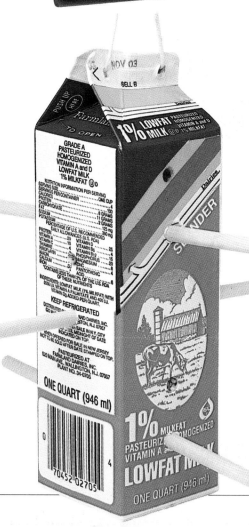

Flower: The flower is the part of a plant that produces seeds.

Gills: Gills are body parts that take oxygen from water. Fish have gills for breathing under water.

Leaf: A leaf is a plant part that changes air, water, and sunlight into food for the plant.

Lens: A lens is a part of an eye that helps animals see things clearly. Each of your eyes has just one lens, but a fly's eye has many lenses.

Lungs: Lungs are body parts that take oxygen from the air. Many animals that live on the land and some animals that live in the water have lungs.

Oxygen: Plants give off oxygen, which is left over when they make their food. Animals need oxygen to live and get it from the air they breathe.